Panda Climbs

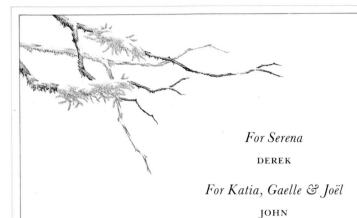

For Serena

DEREK

For Katia, Gaelle & Joël

JOHN

Text copyright © 1984 by Derek Hall
Illustrations copyright © 1984 by John Butler
All rights reserved under International and Pan-American Copyright
Conventions. Published in the United States by Alfred A. Knopf, Inc.,
New York. Originally published in Great Britain by Walker Books Ltd.,
London. Manufactured in Italy 10 9 8 7 6 5 4 3 2 1
First American Edition

Library of Congress Cataloging in Publication Data
Hall, Derek, 1930– Panda climbs. (Growing up)
Summary: Portrays a baby panda in his environment with his parents,
eating, playing, and climbing a tree. 1. Giant panda–Juvenile literature.
[1. Giant panda. 2. Pandas] I. Butler, John, 1952– ill.
II. Title. III. Series: Growing up (Alfred A. Knopf)
QL737.C214H34 1984 599.74′443 83-17462
ISBN 0-394-86502-2 ISBN 0-394-96502-7 (lib. bdg.)

Panda Climbs

By Derek Hall

Illustrations by John Butler

Sierra Club / Alfred A. Knopf

San Francisco   New York

Panda loves to play with his mother. Sometimes she gives him a piggy-back ride and then he feels as tall as a grown-up panda.

Soon it is dinnertime.
The grown-ups eat lots of
bamboo shoots, crunching
the juicy stems. Panda likes
to chew the soft leaves.

The grown-ups eat for such
a long time, they always
fall asleep afterward.
Panda scampers off to play.
He rolls over and over in
the snow and tumbles
down a hill.

When Panda stops at
the bottom he cannot see
his mother anymore.
But he sees a leopard!
Panda is very frightened.

He scrambles over to the
nearest tree and climbs up.
Panda has never climbed before,
and it is so easy! He digs his
claws into the bark and goes
up and up.

Soon he is near the top.
Panda feels so good up here.
And he can see such a long
way over the mountains and
trees and snow of China.

Panda hears his mother
crying. She is looking for him.
He starts to climb down.
But going down is harder
than climbing up, and he slips.
Plop! He lands in the snow.

Panda's mother is so happy.
She gathers him up in her big
furry arms and cuddles him.
It is lovely to be warm and
safe with her again.